THE Regulation STATION

Exploring tools to help manage FEELINGS and EMOTIONS

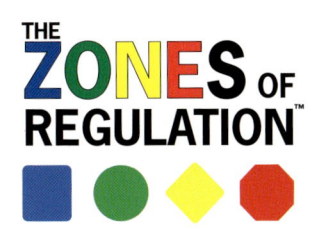

THE ZONES OF REGULATION™

Leah Kuypers and Elizabeth Sautter

Illustrated by Fátima Anaya

25+ YRS! Social Thinking®

Think Social Publishing, Inc., Santa Clara, California
www.socialthinking.com

The Zones of Regulation™
The Regulation Station: Exploring Tools to Help Manage Feelings and Emotions

Written by Leah M. Kuypers, MA Ed. OTR/L and Elizabeth Sautter, MA, CCC-SLP
www.zonesofregulation.com
The Zones of Regulation™ is a trademark belonging to Leah Kuypers.
Copyright © 2021 Think Social Publishing, Inc.
All Rights Reserved except as noted herein.

Outside of the specific use described below, all other reproduction/copying, adaptation, conversion to electronic format, or sharing/distribution of content, through print or electronic means, is not permitted without written permission from Think Social Publishing, Inc. (TSP).

This includes prohibition of any use of any content or materials from this product as part of an adaptation or derivative work you create for posting on a personal or business website, TeachersPayTeachers, YouTube, Pinterest, Facebook, or any other social media or information sharing site in existence now or in the future, whether free or for a fee. Exceptions are made, upon written request, for product reviews, articles, and blogposts.

Think Social Publishing, Inc. (TSP) grants permission to the owner of this book to use and/or adapt content in print or electronic form, **only** for direct in-classroom/school/home or in-clinic use with your own students/clients/children, and with the primary stakeholders in that individual's life, which includes parents/caregivers and direct service personnel. The copyright for any adaptation of content owned by TSP remains with TSP as a derivative work.

Social Thinking, Superflex, The Unthinkables, The Thinkables, and We Thinkers! GPS are trademarks belonging to TSP. The Zones of Regulation is a trademark belonging to Leah Kuypers, a TSP author.

Translation of this product can only be done in accordance with our TRANSLATION POLICY found on our intellectual property website page here: https://www.socialthinking.com/intellectual-property.

And, visit our intellectual property page to find detailed TERMS OF USE information and a DECISION-TREE that cover copyright, trademark, and intellectual property topics and questions governing the use of our materials.

ISBN: 978-1-936943-61-6 (print)
ISBN: 978-1-936943-70-8 (Zones of Regulation 2-Storybook Set ebook)

Think Social Publishing, Inc.
404 Saratoga Avenue, Suite 200
Santa Clara, CA 95050
Tel: (408) 557-8595
Fax: (408) 557-8594

Illustrated by Fátima Anaya
Book design by Megan Jones Design

This book was printed and bound in the United States by Mighty Color Printing.
TSP is a sole source provider of Social Thinking Products in the U.S.
Books may be purchased online at www.socialthinking.com

Dedicated to all the co-regulators out there who are making a difference in the lives of so many children. Keep up the great work.

Thank you to Gabriel, Julian, Daniel, Vivian, and let's not forget Emma for helping us by providing real-life experiences and your advice on how to share this information.

INTRODUCTION AND RECOMMENDED TEACHING

As we learned in the first book, *The Road to Regulation*, our body (including our brain) feels sensations, states of alertness (energy) and emotions. They come and go and are influenced by what is happening around us, what we are thinking about, and how we feel. They are not bad or good but can feel comfortable (happy, excited, or warm) or uncomfortable (sad, scared, or over-heated). We use the word "feelings" to describe sensations, emotions, and our states of alertness throughout this storybook. To recap, here is a review of the important ideas that we learned about in the first book.

Feelings come in different sizes, intensities, and levels of energy. To make this easy to talk and think about, we can categorize them into four simple, colored categories that we call The Zones of Regulation.

- ■ The **BLUE ZONE** is used to describe low states of alertness and down feelings, such as when a person feels sad, tired, sick, or bored.

- ● The **GREEN ZONE** is used to describe a calm state of alertness. A person may be described as happy, focused, content, or ready to learn when in the Green Zone. This is the zone where optimal learning occurs.

- ◆ The **YELLOW ZONE** is used to describe when our energy is higher and emotions get a little bigger, making it a bit harder to regulate. A person may be experiencing stress, frustration, anxiety, excitement, silliness, the wiggles, or nervousness when in the Yellow Zone.

- ⬢ The **RED ZONE** is used to describe extremely high energy and intense feelings. A person may be feeling elated, anger, rage, devastation, out of control, or terrified when in the Red Zone.

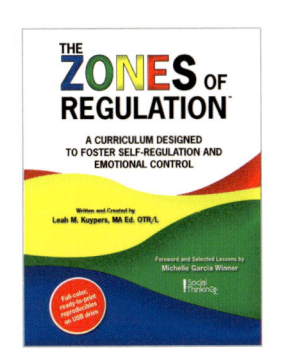

The Zones of Regulation® Curriculum

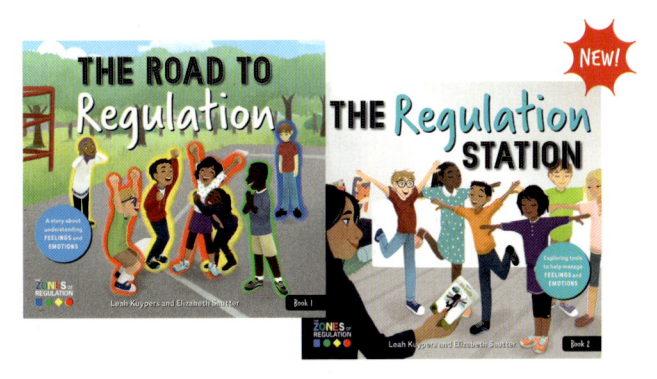

The Road to Regulation (Book 1) and *The Regulation Station* (Book 2)

Tools to Try Cards for Kids

These two children's books were created to provide an easy, kid-friendly way to introduce and support The Zones of Regulation framework, for children developmental ages 5 to 11. They are meant to be used in conjunction with lessons from the curriculum book, *The Zones of Regulation* (Kuypers, 2011). They are a supplement to, not a replacement for, the in-depth lessons found in *The Zones of Regulation* curriculum book. The *Tools to Try Cards for Kids* deck is designed to be used in conjunction with the storybooks and curriculum. *The Road to Regulation* is the first of two stories that starts the conversation and introduces the first steps within the Zones framework. This book, *The Regulation Station*, continues the story with the same characters on an adventure to learn how to use tools and strategies to regulate their Zones. Just like the first book, this book can be used in multiple ways: read to a whole classroom of students, used as a therapy tool, read as a bedtime story, or for children to pick up and read on their own. When reading this storybook, take the time to discuss the situations and help children reflect on and process times when they have been in similar situations and how they might have felt. See the Extend the Learning section on page 76 for guided questions and curriculum references, followed by a vocabulary list, "dos and don'ts," and sample *Tools to Try* cards.

Enjoy,

LEAH and **ELIZABETH**

"Well, that was a long day. I'm glad to be home. I'm exhausted," announces Gabriel's dad as he walks in the door.

Gabriel looks at Nana with a knowing look, both saying out loud, "He's in the Blue Zone."

"What's the Blue Zone?" Gabriel's dad asks.

7

The ZON[E]

Blue Zone

- SAD
- BORED
- TIRED
- SICK

The **BLUE ZONE** is when we have lower energy, down feelings, and we might feel sad, sick, tired, or bored.

Green Zon[e]

- HAPPY
- FOCUSED
- READY TO LEARN
- OKAY

The **GREEN ZONE** is when we have calm energy and may feel focused, happy, okay, or ready to learn.

> It's something we're learning about in school. Let me show you. It explains the Blue, Green, Yellow, and Red Zones. The Zones are an easy way to think and talk about how we are feeling.

...s of Regulation

Yellow Zone

- FRUSTRATED
- WORRIED
- EXCITED
- SILLY

Red Zone

- ELATED
- PANICKED
- ANGRY
- TERRIFIED

The **YELLOW ZONE** is when we have more energy and feelings get a little stronger. We might feel excited, silly, frustrated, or worried.

The **RED ZONE** is when our feelings and energy are so big that we may feel like we might burst, such as when we feel angry, terrifi...

Throughout dinner, Gabriel notices his dad still looking tired. He gets an idea and says to his dad, "I know what will help you with your Blue Zone . . . GAME NIGHT!!"

"I'll make popcorn!" offers Alma, Gabriel's sister, feeling excited. "I'll grab some games," says Nana. Gabriel chimes in, "Game night has me feeling in the Green Zone."

"That does sound like fun. Game night it is," says Gabriel's dad.

11

12

"We made a great team tonight. That was fun, but it's been a long day. Sweet dreams Gabriel," his dad whispers.

Gabriel is so tired in the Blue Zone. His body feels heavy and he can barely keep his eyes open. He is glad to lie down and get some sleep. He quickly slips into a dream . . .

Gabriel's dream lands him on a bus with his friends. He hears a familiar voice make an announcement, "Welcome to the Road to Regulation field trip. Please sit down and lower your voices. It's hard to drive this bus with all this noise." Most of the kids keep goofing around and talking except Vivian, who tries to contain her laughter.

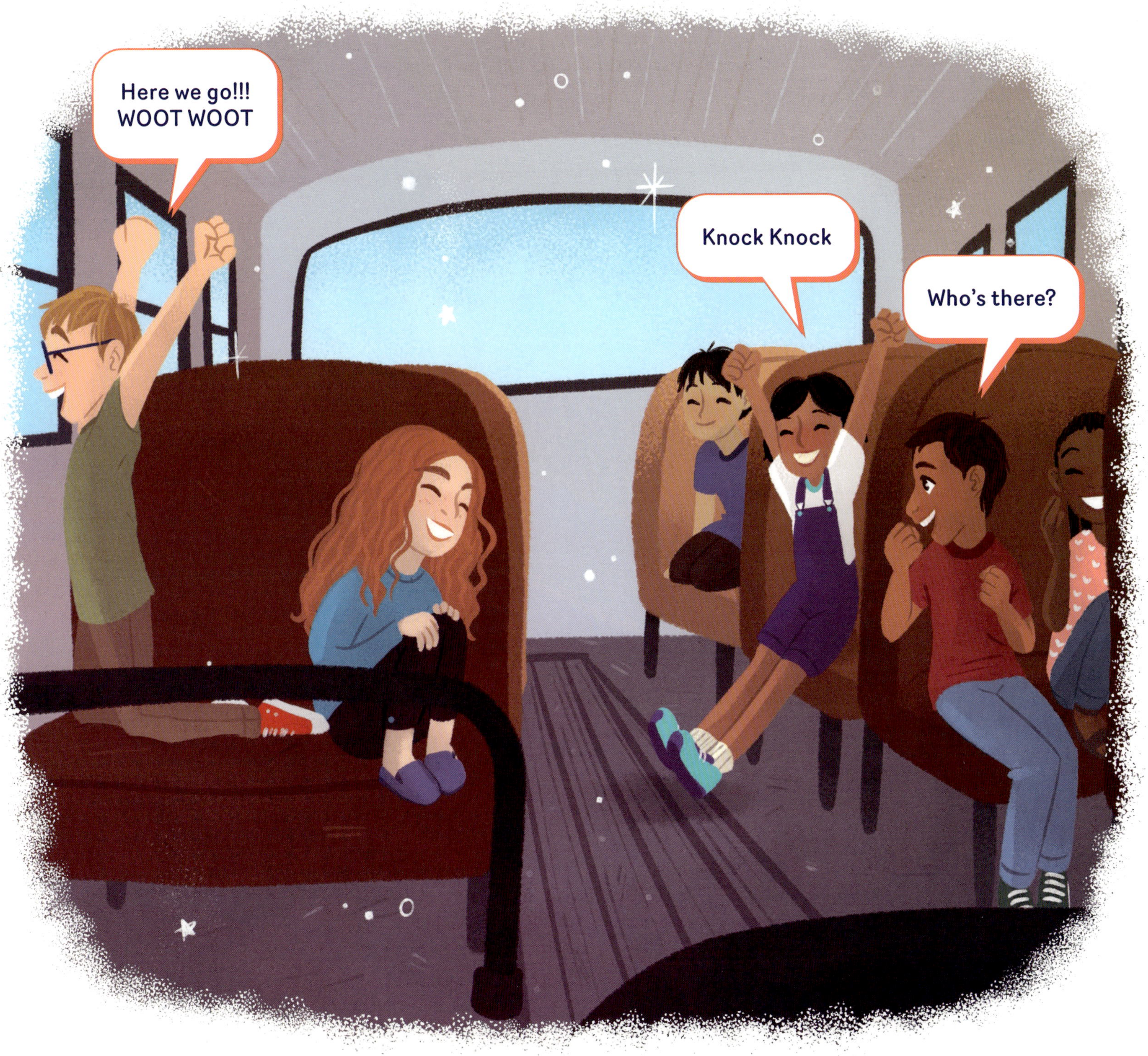
Here we go!!!
WOOT WOOT
Knock Knock
Who's there?

There is a lot of energy on this bus! I have to pull over and STOP.

All the kids were startled by the bus jerking to a stop. What was even more shocking to see was the sight of Mr. Daniel standing up from the driver's seat with a frustrated look on his face. Gabriel couldn't imagine what might happen next.

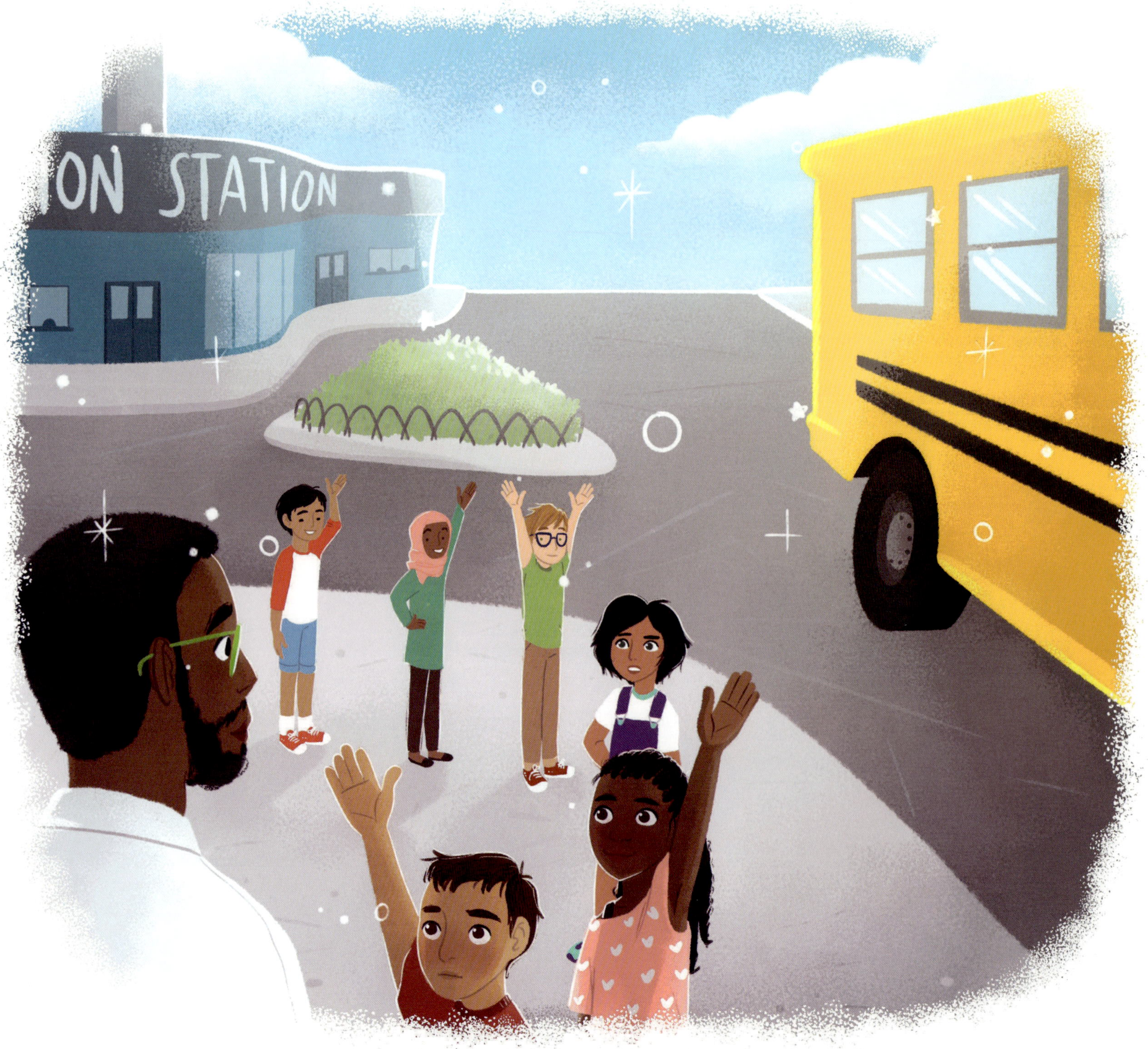
ON STATION

After the kids file off the bus, Mr. Daniel takes a deep breath and checks in with everyone. "All that energy on the bus was so distracting. It felt unsafe for me to keep driving. On the Road to Regulation, we have been practicing how to listen to our bodies and notice our feelings and Zones. Mine was telling me I was getting close to the Red Zone so I had to stop. Take a moment to notice how you feel. Anybody else having a hard time regulating their Zone?" Many kids raise their hands.

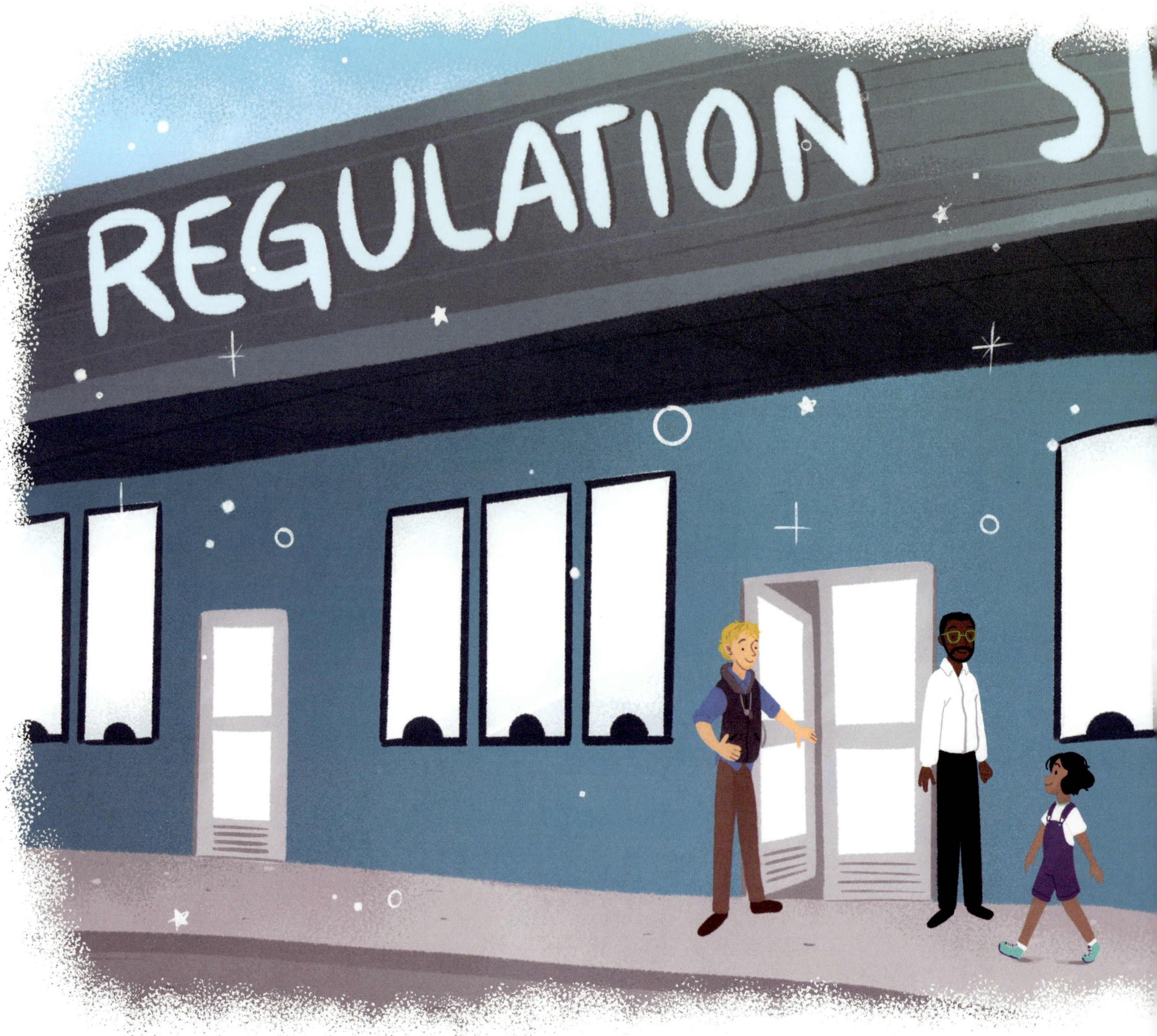
REGULATION

"Thankfully we're at the *Regulation Station*. It's always here when you need it, and boy do we need this now. And look, it's Mr. Anthony. He's going to help us explore some tools inside," says Mr. Daniel.

Welcome to the Regulation Station! I'm glad you are here. Let's check-in to get started. Think about how you're feeling and press the colored button to let me know what Zone you're in as you enter the station.

23

"Funny seeing you here Mr. Anthony. I'm feeling silly in the Yellow Zone," says Suhana as she pushes the Yellow Zone button and walks into the Regulation Station.

Julian springs out of the line, jumping over the turnstile while hitting the Red Zone button. "I'm feeling wild in the Red Zone!" announces Julian. "Come on in, you're in the right place!" Mr. Anthony assures him.

"I'm so glad you all stopped here because this station is unlike any other. It is filled with tools which are activities that you can do to help you regulate your Zones. Ms. Lee is also here to help out. Let's explore some tools to see what you think about them. Do they help you feel more in control of your Zone?" asks Mr. Anthony.

What Zone are you in?

Julian races ahead of the other kids with excited energy pumping through him. A path of pinwheels catches his eye and Mr. Anthony is at the end holding out a big shiny pinwheel for him. "This is for you," he says. "Take a deep breath and slowly blow out to make the pinwheel turn."

Julian fills his lungs with air and blows out to spin the pinwheel. "Now try to keep it moving with more deep breaths. Are you noticing any changes to how you feel?" asks Mr. Anthony.

"Yep, that does help me to slow down," replies Julian. Mr. Anthony goes on to explain that deep breathing may be a tool that Julian finds helpful to manage his energy.

Feeling annoyed in the Yellow Zone from all the shenanigans on the bus, Vivian's eyes popped open, amazed to see an art table in the Regulation Station. She knew coloring was just what she needed to let go of her frustration. Her teacher, Ms. Lee, came over to check in with her.

What a beautiful drawing. You look so peaceful.
Yeah, I love doing art."
That is awesome. Art might make a great tool for you!

"Thank goodness!" Suhana exclaims as she runs toward the monkey bars. She knows this will help her get out the wiggles that had built up while riding on the bus.

"Hey Mr. Anthony, watch this!" Suhana calls out as she swings across the monkey bars.

Mr. Anthony smiles and says, "Looks like you're onto something. You found a tool to help your body feel more comfortable. Isn't it cool that something as fun as playing on the monkey bars can also be a regulation tool?"

I don't know about you, but that bus ride felt overwhelming. It's fun to laugh and joke, but sometimes it can be taken too far and make others feel uncomfortable. This is what seemed to happen on the bus. Want to join me in using one of my favorite tools, Wall Pushes? It helps me feel more in control of my Zone.

I guess so.

"Come on, let's push as hard as we can," encouraged Mr. Daniel. Together they pushed against the wall with all their might, the silliness leaving Gabriel's body. Suddenly, they hear a cracking noise and feel the wall give way. . . .

Before they know it, the wall topples over. Gabriel and Mr. Daniel find themselves feeling shocked as they land in a pile of bricks. They quickly realize they're both okay and start to laugh together. They brush themselves off as they head back to the bus.

Calling all passengers traveling on The Road to Regulation. The bus will be departing in 5 minutes!

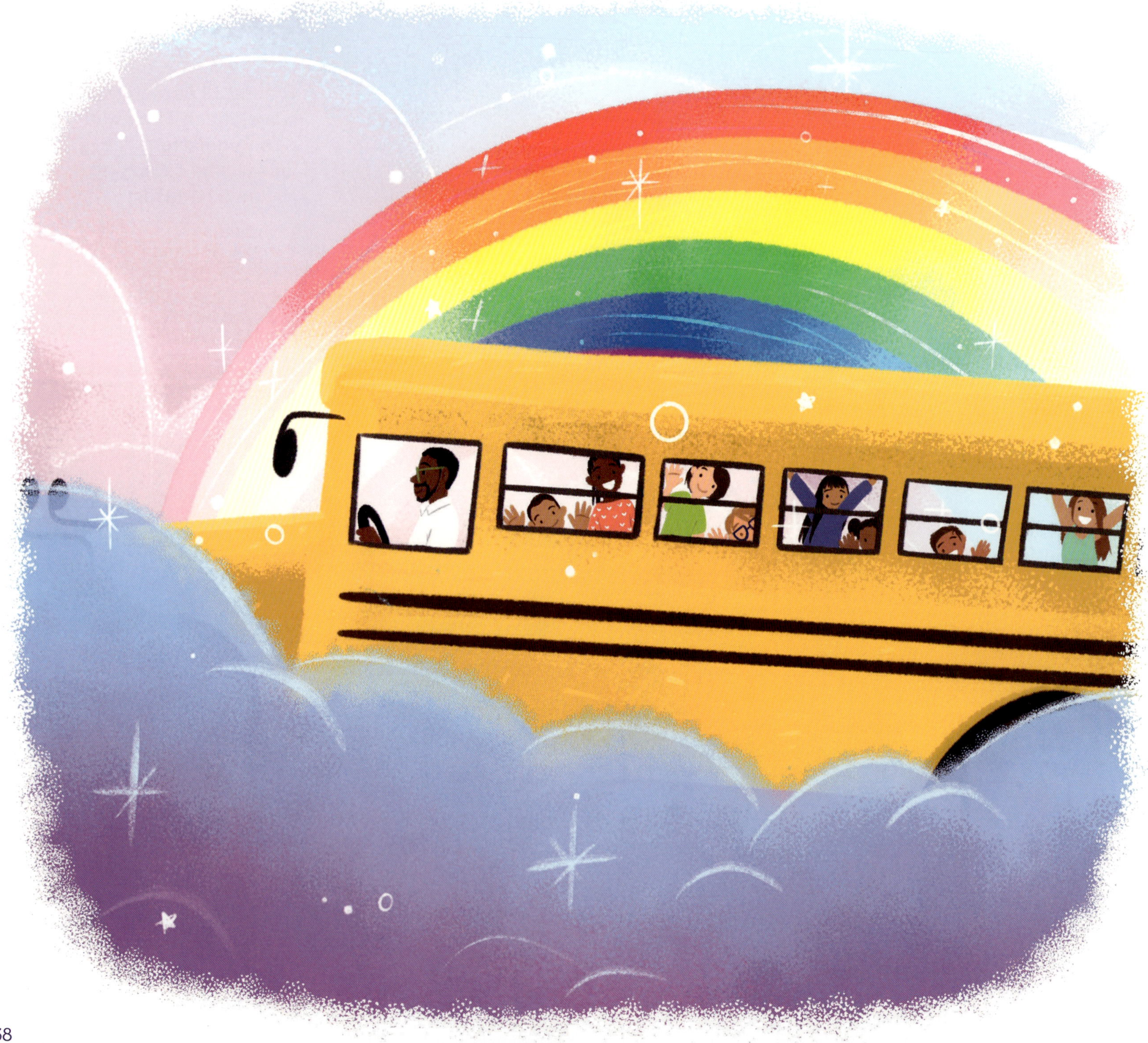

"Hold on tight, our journey along the Road to Regulation isn't over just yet," says Mr. Daniel. "Now that we all had the chance to try some tools to help us regulate, we are moving onto our next stop, Destination Regulation." Gabriel and his classmates look out the bus windows in awe as the bus floats like a balloon off the road, up toward a rainbow in the sky.

Still half asleep, Gabriel hears his dad's voice, "Time to wake up." His brain feels fuzzy as he is coming out of his dream. "Not yet, Mr. Daniel. We are on our way to Destination Regulation," he mumbles.

"What? Gabriel, I think you're still dreaming," his dad says. Gabriel rolls over, opening his eyes to see his dad standing above him. "Dad, I had a crazy dream." He goes on to tell his dad all about the wild bus ride and the Regulation Station.

Gabriel continues to think about his dream as he gets ready and heads to school.

41

"Hello kids! Today we are going to talk about tools. Can one of you tell me what these tools help us with?"

"Build and fix things."

A few weeks later at school, Mr. Daniel comes back to visit the classroom.

Next, Mr. Daniel pulls out kitchen tools including a spatula, whisk, and measuring spoons. "What do these tools help us do?" Another student answers, "They help us cook and bake things."

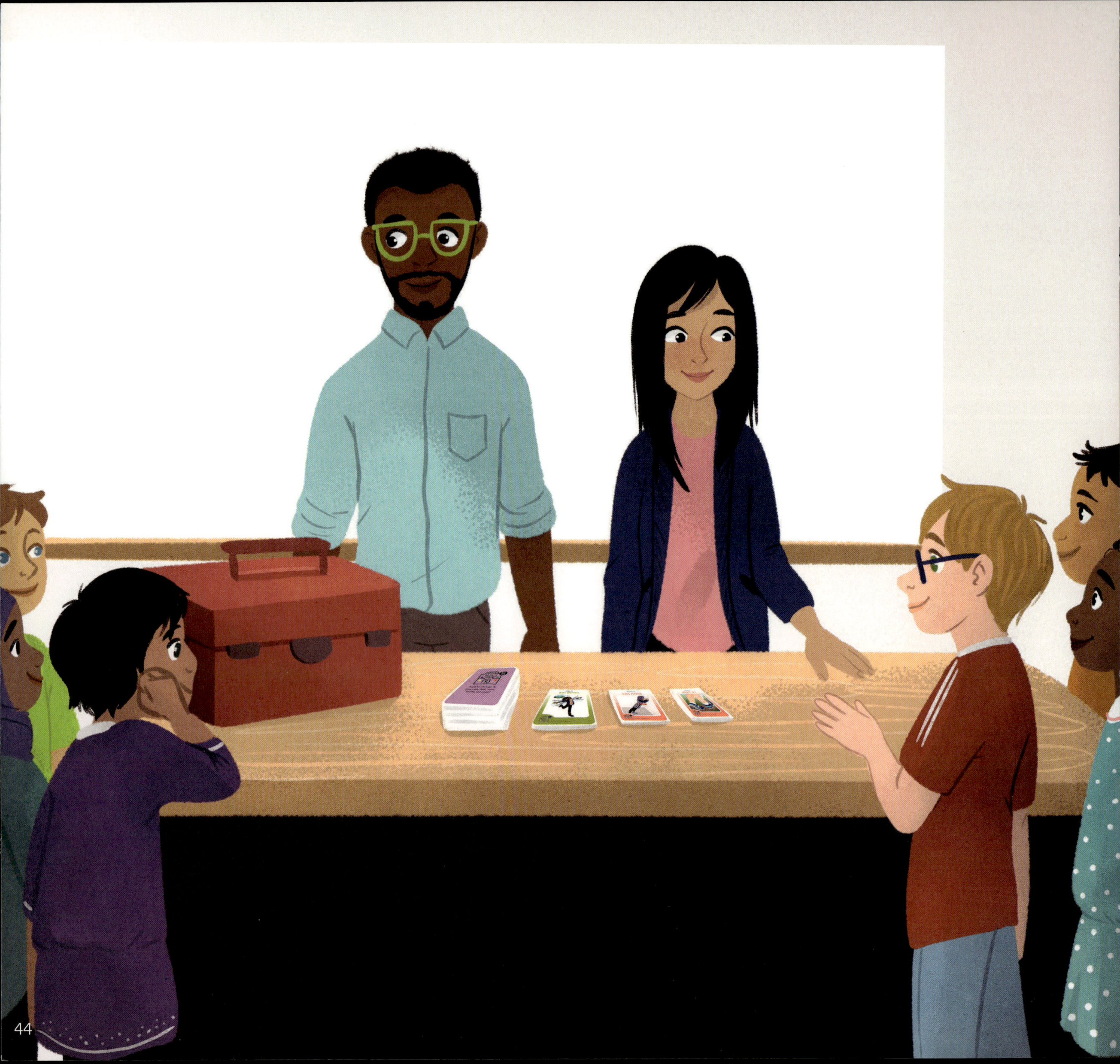

Next, Mr. Daniel pulls out a deck of cards from his toolbox. He displays them for the students to see as he reads the tools' names aloud. "Bird Breaths, Wall Pushes, Walk It Out," he says. "Any ideas what these tools can help us with?"

Gabriel has a flashback to his dream of riding the bus along the Road to Regulation. He remembers the stop at the Regulation Station and knows he has the answer. He raises his hand. "These tools help us REGULATE!" he exclaims.

"Exactly! We use tools to help us do many different types of things, including manage our feelings and behavior," Mr. Daniel says.

Mr. Daniel goes on to say, "Not only that, they can also help us get our jobs and responsibilities done. Let's discuss some of your jobs and responsibilities as students while at school?" The students were quick to raise their hands and share their ideas.

Do our school work.
Listen to my teacher.
Help clean up.
Be kind to others.
How about participate in discussions?

Next, Mr. Daniel explains to the class how tools help in each of the four Zones.

Blue Zone

COMFORT
ENERGIZE
REST

Green Zone

GO

■ **BLUE ZONE** tools help us rest up, get energized, focus, or provide comfort.

● **GREEN ZONE** tools help us with everyday needs to feel good, healthy, and stay organized.

Yellow Zone

**SLOW DOWN
CAUTION**

Red Zone

**STOP
PAUSE**

◆ **YELLOW ZONE** tools help us feel calmer and in control.

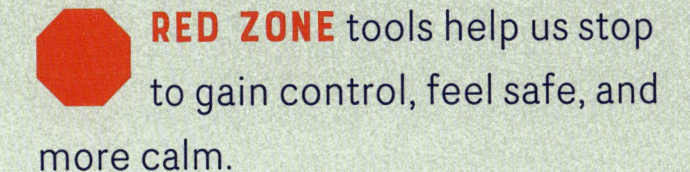

⬢ **RED ZONE** tools help us stop to gain control, feel safe, and more calm.

Mr. Daniel explains, "Let's review where we are on the Road to Regulation. First, we spent time learning to notice the signals in our body to understand how we are feeling, and then identifying what Zone we are in. Once we know what Zone we're in, we have a better idea of what tool to use if we need to regulate. Ms. Lee and I are excited to share some more tools to help us with this third step."

STEP 1
How do I feel?
STEP 2
What Zone am I in?
STEP 3
Do I need a tool to regulate? Which one?

52

Ms. Lee joins Mr. Daniel in the front of the classroom. "The tools will be valuable for regulating our feelings and actions to help us feel safe and comfortable around each other at school and home. I will be teaching a *Tool of the Week*, which we will be practicing every day," Ms. Lee added. "Tools support each of us in different ways. One of you may find that the tool helps you in the Yellow Zone, another may find that the same tool is helpful in the Blue Zone. We are going to make time to practice using different tools so you can figure out what tools work for you across your different Zones."

"The first Tool of the Week is Bird Breaths," Ms. Lee says, displaying a card illustrating Bird Breaths to the students.

"Imagine you are a bird soaring in the sky as you stretch your arms out like wings.

Breathe in deeply while raising up your arms over your head.

Close your eyes and imagine what you would see below.

Slowly breathe out as you bring your arms back down."

55

That helped me feel calm. I think it would make a good Yellow Zone tool.
Blue Zone
Green Zone
Red Zone

"Do you think the tool, Bird Breaths, might help you in one or more of your Zones?" asks Ms. Lee.

She passes out the *Zones Tools Worksheet* and shows her students how to record a tool in the Zone it might help them with. "This will help you keep track of which tools you might want to use again," she explained.

"Now let's put our worksheets in our Zones folders and line up for recess. Have fun and remember that our tools aren't just for the classroom. We can use them anywhere, including in your home, in the community, and even at recess!"

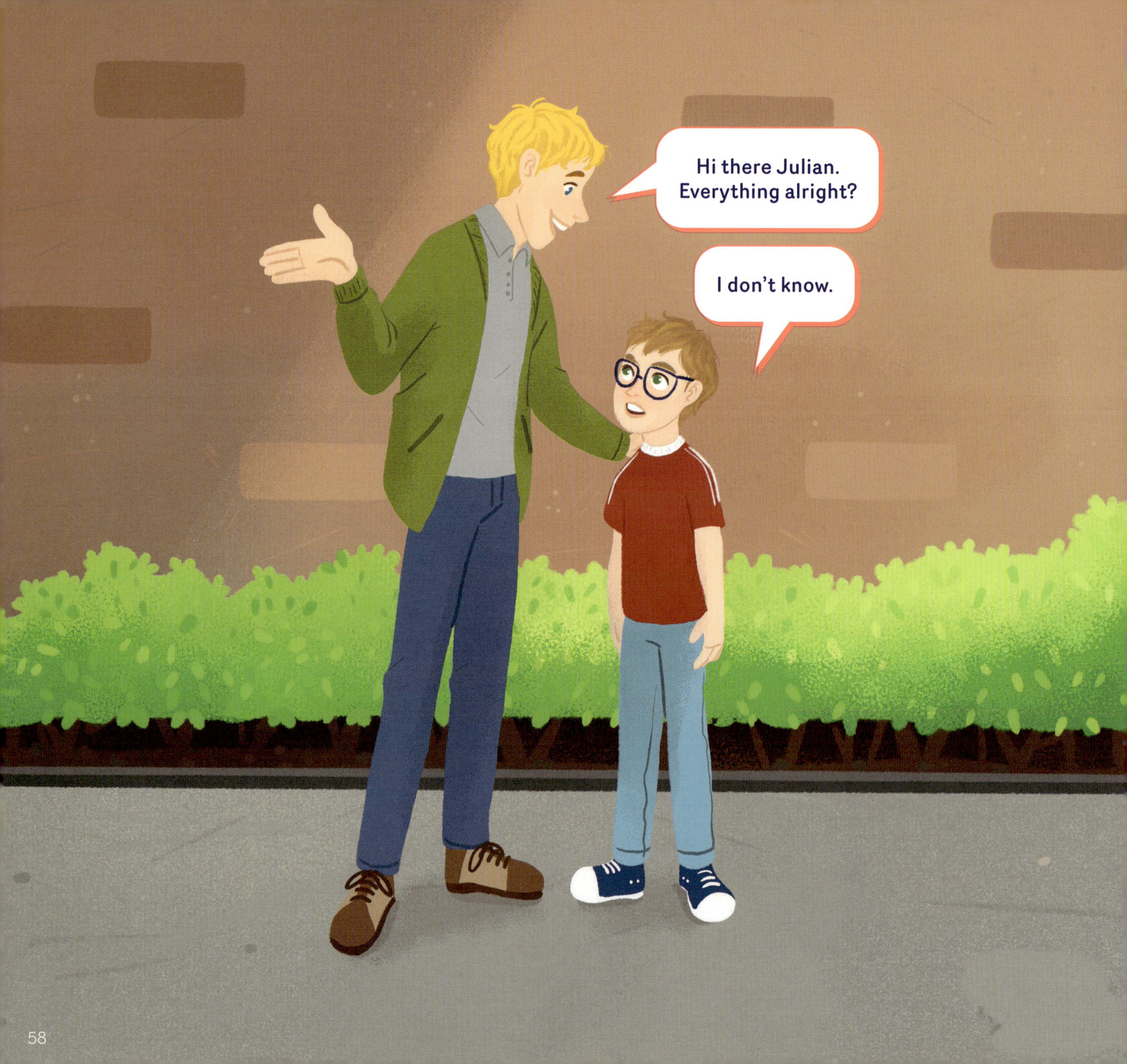
Hi there Julian.
Everything alright?
I don't know.

At recess, Mr. Anthony notices Julian walking with his head down and his body moving slowly. Mr. Anthony suggests they check-in with the Zones.

"I guess I'm feeling bored in the Blue Zone. I don't know what to do," says Julian.

Mr. Anthony replies, "I hear you buddy. How 'bout we Walk it Out while we look around to see what your schoolmates are up to? Think about if noticing what others are doing will help you choose what you want to do. Do you think Walk it Out might make a good tool for your Blue Zone?"

"I'll give it a try," says Julian, and he walks over to the four square game.

"It's not fair. I just got in!"

Playing four square, Suhana is upset that she gets out right after she got into the game. Her body feels restless having to wait in line again and the frustration pulses through her.

Vivian sees that Suhana is upset and says, "Sorry you got out so quickly. Maybe the Bird Breath tool that we learned today would help?" After a few Bird Breaths, Suhana feels herself slow down. She smiles at Vivian and thanks her.

The whistle blows, alerting the kids to line up to go back to class. Gabriel thought it was his day to be line leader and races to the front but another student is already there saying it's his turn. Gabriel feels annoyed in the Yellow Zone and is worried that he won't get his turn as line leader.

Mr. Anthony senses the heightened energy from Gabriel and his classmates lining up and suggests they all try Wall Pushes as a tool.

Wall Pushes are a tool that helps me slow down when I'm in the Yellow Zone, but can help in other Zones too. What do you all think about the Wall Pushes?
I was already feeling good, but I think it will help me be even more focused in class.
Wow, I used two tools at recess and now I feel great. I needed them.
Well, my body feels calmer but I'm still a little bummed.
Maybe we should do these every day when we come in from recess so we are good to go.

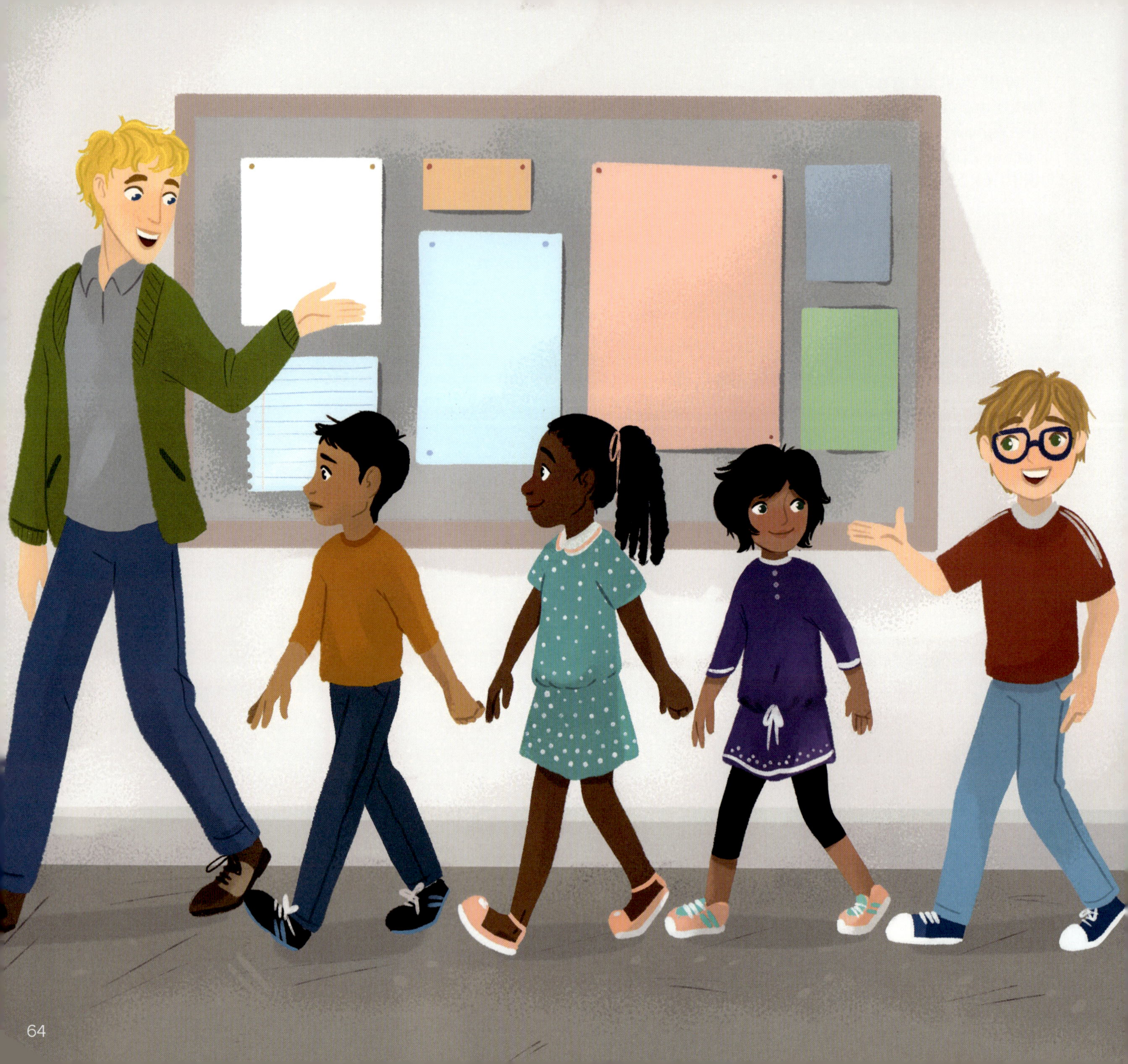

As the kids walk back to class, they talk about how the Wall Pushes made them feel. It is becoming clear that the same tool can help in different Zones and in different situations.

"Welcome back," says Ms. Lee. "I was just finishing setting this up as another tool—or group of tools—to explore." The kids stop to take a look before they make their way to their seats. Once Gabriel sees the new tool area, he has a feeling it is just what he needs and asks if he could give it a try. Ms. Lee agrees and goes on to tell the class, "Remember, tools help us to meet our goals and get our jobs done. They don't get in the way."

67

Gabriel was so relieved to have a place to chill out for a minute to help him manage his Yellow Zone.

"What should we call this new comfy area where we can go to regulate our Zones?" Ms. Lee asks. Gabriel is listening and thinks back to his dream. It all started to come together for him on this Road to Regulation journey.

"How about the Regulation Station?" Gabriel volunteers with a big smile stretched across his face.

Ms. Lee smiles back and announces to the class that they will all get a turn to try out the classroom's newest tool area, the Regulation Station.

69

"Thanks Ms. Lee, the Regulation Station was just the ticket I needed to move on with my day. Now I know how it feels to experience destination regulation."

"I've never heard of that but it sounds like a good place to be."

Ms. Lee winks at Gabriel and says, "Alright class, let's review our Zones journey."

"In Step 1, we learned to pay attention to our body's signals, feelings, and levels of energy.

In Step 2, we figured out what Zone we are in.

Now in Step 3, we're thinking about if and how we need to regulate ourselves in our Zone. Do we need to STOP/PAUSE, SLOW DOWN, REST UP/ENERGIZE or are we good to GO?

Each week we will continue to explore tools we can use to change our Zone or regulate ourselves to be more comfortable and controlled within it.

Step 4 is to use the tool to regulate our Zone, and as Gabriel said, this leads us to our destination on the Road to Regulation."

The Road to

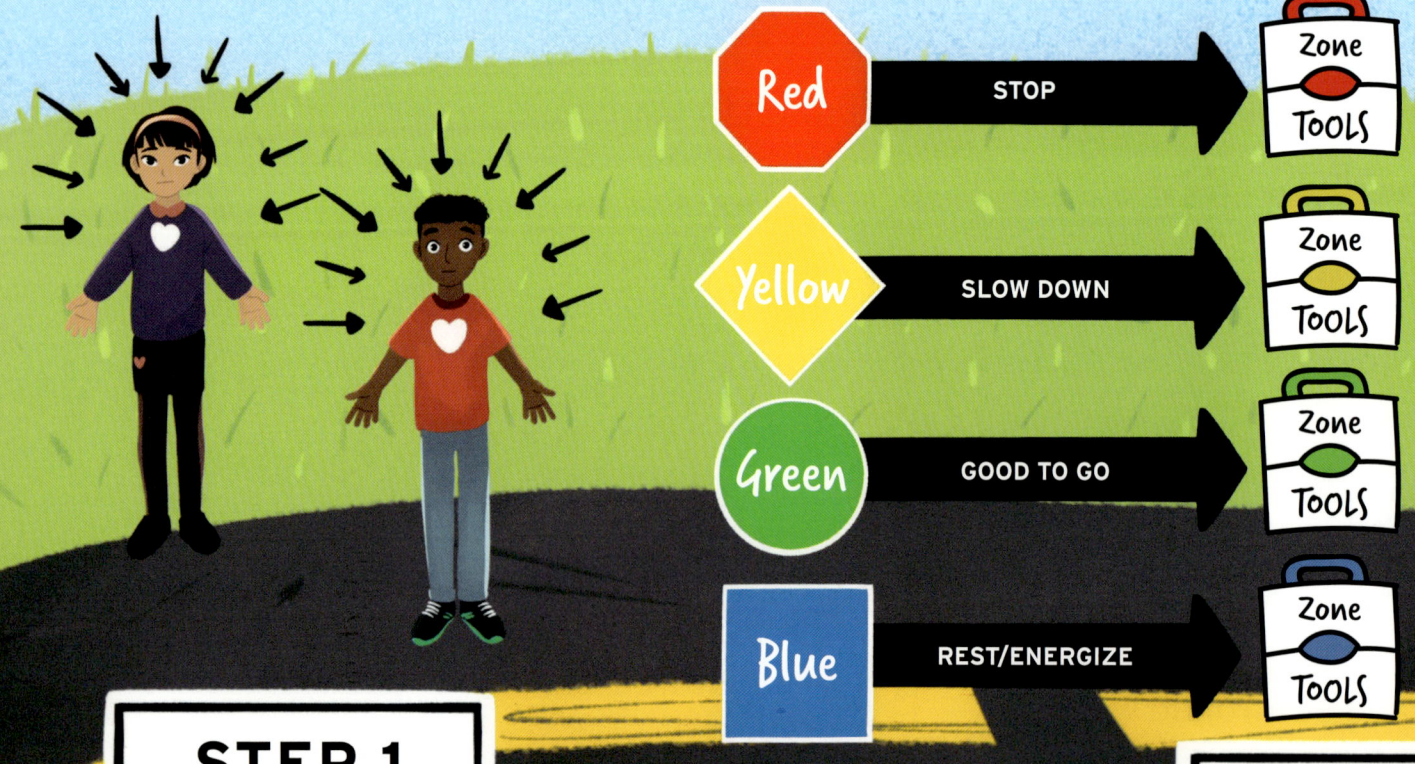

Red	STOP	Zone Tools
Yellow	SLOW DOWN	Zone Tools
Green	GOOD TO GO	Zone Tools
Blue	REST/ENERGIZE	Zone Tools

STEP 1
How do I feel?

STEP 2
What Zone am I in?

STEP 3
Do I need a tool to regulate? Which one?

Regulation

I CAN...
- Have fun
- Do my job
- Focus
- Be in control
- Join in
- Solve the problem

Welcome to Destination Regulation

STEP 4
Use the tool.

I'm excited to figure out which tools I can use at home to help me in my Zones and share that with my family. Maybe I'll even dream about it tonight when I go to bed!
You have NO IDEA!

75

EXTEND THE LEARNING: TIPS FOR FACILITATORS

Continue with the same conversations that were started with *The Road to Regulation*, and consider the additional ideas below to use these books to teach your child(ren) about The Zones of Regulation and understand their feelings and behaviors.

While reading the story, pause periodically on the pages to discuss the following:

1. How are the characters feeling in different situations and what Zone are they in? How can you tell? (Review of *The Road to Regulation* and Chapter 3 from *The Zones of Regulation*)

2. Find an example in the book of when a character was regulating their Zone and their behavior was expected in a situation. Make a guess about how those around the character felt about their behavior in that situation. Find an example of when a character was not regulating their Zone and their behavior was unexpected. How did others around them feel? (Lessons 3 and 5)

3. On pages 46–47, the characters brainstormed some of their jobs at school. What are some of your jobs as a student, member of your family, and community? How could Zones tools help you with these jobs?

4. Referring to pages 48–49 in *The Regulation Station* (illustration of the 4 Zones with tool ideas), ask the child(ren) to brainstorm an example of a tool that might help them regulate in each of the Blue, Green, Yellow, and Red Zones. (Chapter 4 in *The Zones of Regulation*)

5. Explore the situations that unfold in the book. Ask the child(ren) if they have ideas of other tools that may help the characters regulate their Zones. Do they have tools they would use in similar situations to help them regulate their own Zone? (Chapter 4 and Lesson 14)

VOCABULARY

The Zones of Regulation: A way to think about all the different ways we feel on the inside and sort those feelings into four colored Zones. This gives us an easy way to identify, talk about, and regulate our feelings.

Blue Zone: Used to describe low levels of energy and down feelings, such as when a person feels sad, tired, sick, or bored.

Green Zone: Used to describe when we feel calm and in control. A person may be described as happy, focused, content, or ready to learn when in the Green Zone. This is the Zone where optimal learning occurs.

Yellow Zone: Used to describe when our energy is higher and feelings get a little bigger, making it a bit harder to regulate. A person may be experiencing stress, frustration, anxiety, excitement, silliness, the wiggles, or nervousness when in the Yellow Zone.

Red Zone: Used to describe extremely high energy and intense feelings. A person may be feeling elated, anger, rage, devastation, out of control, or terrified when in the Red Zone.

Feelings: The signals, emotions, and energy within our body.

Regulate: Being able to manage our feelings and behaviors in a situation in order to keep us and others comfortable while also helping us do what we need to do. This may require us to use tools/strategies to help us.

Signals/Sensations: Information from our body that helps us figure out how we feel.

Toolbox: A collection of tools and strategies that can be used to help us regulate our Zones.

Tools/Strategies: Thoughts, actions, or activities we can do to change our Zone/feeling or regulate ourselves to be more comfortable and controlled within it.

Dos	Don'ts
✓ Do use this book after *The Road to Regulation* has been already introduced and in conjunction with the lessons in *The Zones of Regulation* curriculum for deeper teaching and extending activities and applications.	✗ Don't have the storybook be children's only exposure to The Zones of Regulation framework. Don't skip reading *The Road to Regulation* first.
✓ Do teach a variety of tools over time for children to explore. Allow ample time for children to practice their tools when in calmer states. Once familiar with a variety of tools, encourage students to individualize their Zones tools in their toolbox based upon what they feel works for them. This is to increase motivation and flexibility.	✗ Don't expect children to be able to use tools in heightened states of alertness/energy (e.g. when they are upset), or as soon as they are introduced. They will need lots of practice while in calm states to build familiarity with tools before they are able to use them in real time to regulate their Zones. This timing will be unique to each child, some needing a lot more support than others in order to do so.
✓ Do model using tools yourself, highlighting how the different tools from your toolbox helps you regulate your four Zones. It is important to create a climate where it is safe to be learning how to regulate, and where even the adults are working on this skill.	✗ Don't simply put up tool visuals and expect children to use tools to regulate their Zones. How to use tools must be taught and modeled before we can expect children to demonstrate learning.
✓ Do acknowledge when children make an attempt to try a tool, even if it doesn't work in that moment. It is likely a step in the right direction. Praise for effort and allow time later for reflection on how the tool is working.	✗ Don't force children to use specific tools or ones to which they may not have access. Also, ensure that no tools have a negative association, such as calling a "time-out chair" a tool.

TOOLS TO TRY FOR KIDS SAMPLE CARDS

Photocopy the tool cards and keep them handy to practice and use when you need to regulate your Zones.

ACTIVITY 1: **WALL PUSHES** (see pages 62-63)

MOVE IT

WALL PUSHES

The Zones of Regulation™

MOVE IT

WALL PUSHES

1. Face a wall or sturdy surface and stand a couple of steps away.
2. Place both hands against the wall.
3. Lean into the wall with both hands.
4. Try to push with all your might.

How do you feel?

What Zone would this help in? 🟦 🟩 🟨 🟥

Find more tools in the *Tools to Try Cards for Kids* deck available at: www.socialthinking.com

ACTIVITY 2: **BIRD BREATH** (see pages 54-55)

FEEL IT
BIRD BREATH

The Zones of Regulation™

FEEL IT
BIRD BREATH

1. Imagine you are a bird in the sky as you stretch your arms out like wings.
2. Breathe in deeply while raising up your arms over your head.
3. Close your eyes and imagine what you would see below.
4. Slowly breathe out as you bring your arms back down.

How do you feel?

What Zone would this help in?

Find more tools in the *Tools to Try Cards for Kids* deck available at: www.socialthinking.com

ACTIVITY 3: **WALK IT OUT** (see pages 58–59)

MOVE IT
WALK IT OUT

The Zones of Regulation™

MOVE IT
WALK IT OUT

1. Ask an adult if you can go for a short walk.
2. As you are walking, notice your feet on the ground.
3. Notice how your arms swing with each step.
4. Then notice your breath going in and out with each step.

How do you feel?

What Zone would this help in? 🟦 🟩 🟨 🟥

81

ZONES AND OTHER RELATED PRODUCTS

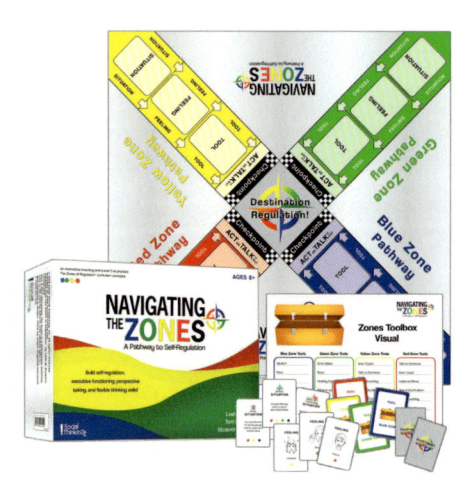

Navigating The Zones

Zones Posters

Advanced Pack: Cards to Extend Play with Navigating The Zones

Tools to Try Cards for Tweens & Teens

New Road to Regulation poster and strategy cards for tweens and teens—Available now!

The Zones of Regulation integrates some core concepts from the Social Thinking® Methodology. See www.socialthinking.com to learn more about these supplemental resources.

AGES 4–7

AGES 4–10

Whole Body Listening Larry at Home!, and *at School!*, 2nd Edition

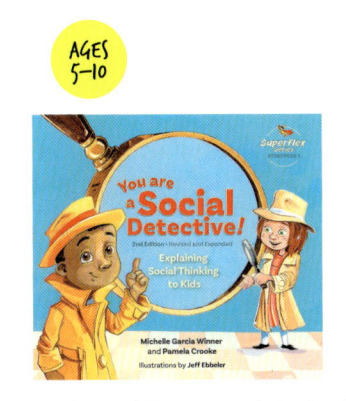

We Thinkers! Series: Volume 1, *Social Explorers* and Volume 2, *Social Problem Solvers*

AGES 5–10

AGES 5–10

AGES 9–12

You Are a Social Detective!, 2nd edition
New, Expanded, and Revised!

Superflex Curriculum

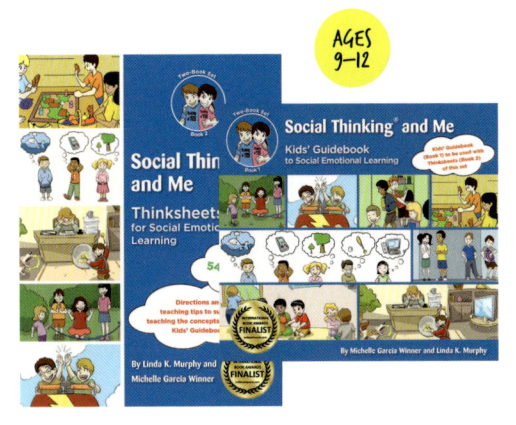

Social Thinking® and Me (two-book set)

ABOUT THE AUTHORS

Leah Kuypers, MA Ed., OTR/L, is the creator of The Zones of Regulation, a framework designed to foster self-regulation. She is the author of the book and apps by the same name, as well as co-creator of *Navigating The Zones* and the *Advanced Pack*. Leah provides trainings and consultation to districts, professionals, and caregivers on regulation and challenging behavior and conducts workshops on The Zones of Regulation framework to groups around the world. Explore her webinars and trainings on her website, www.zonesofregulation.com. She resides in Minneapolis, Minnesota, with her husband, son, daughter, and their dog.

Elizabeth Sautter, MA, CCC-SLP, specializes in social and emotional learning, is the co-owner of Communication Works, a private practice in California, and is the founder of Make Social and Emotional Learning Stick! (www.makesociallearningstick.com) where she blogs and shares resources from her books and online parenting course. Elizabeth is the author of *Make Social and Emotional Learning Stick!*, 2nd edition (2020) and is the co-author of the *Whole Body Listening Larry* books with Kristen Wilson. She presents around the country and beyond on her work and also is a trainer in The Zones of Regulation collaborative.